W9-BZZ-482

Everything You Need to Know

WHEN A
PARENT IS
IN JAIL

Life in prison is very structured and controlled.

• THE NEED TO KNOW LIBRARY •

Everything You Need to Know

WHEN A PARENT IS IN JAIL

Stephanie St. Pierre

THE ROSEN PUBLISHING GROUP, INC.
NEW YORK

Published in 1994 by The Rosen Publishing Group, Inc.
29 East 21st Street, New York, NY 10010

First Edition
Copyright 1994 by The Rosen Publishing Group, Inc.

Manufactured in the United States of America.

Library of Congress Cataloging-in-Publication Data

St. Pierre, Stephanie.
    Everything you need to know when a parent is in jail / Stephanie
St. Pierre. — 1st ed.
        p.   cm.
    Includes bibliographical references and index.
ISBN 0-8239-1526-3
    1. Children of prisoners—United States—Juvenile literature.
2. Prisoners—United States—Family relationships—Juvenile literature.
3. Prisons—United States—Juvenile literature. [1. Prisons. 2. Prisoners.
3. Parent and child] I. Title.
HV8886.U5S69 1993
362.7—dc20   93-32040
                                           CIP
                                           AC

Contents

Introduction

If you have a parent who is serving time in prison, you are probably already aware of many of the difficulties that you face. You know that it is hard to explain your family situation to other people. Whether your parent committed a serious crime or a minor one, there are people who will treat *you* differently because of that. This is a hard thing for the family of an imprisoned person to have to deal with every day. It isn't fair for the child of a prisoner to suffer, but the truth is, you will not live the same life that you did before your parent was arrested. Your family may have money problems. You may have to move. Old friends may not be as friendly as they once were. Even relatives may keep their distance from you and your family.

However painful it is to live with the effects of your parent's imprisonment, you may miss the parent who is serving time. In the best of situations, you will only be able to see your parent once in a while. In most cases, you will have very limited contact with your parent until he or she is free again, and that may be a long, long time in the future. In fact, by the time your parent is out of jail, you may be an adult yourself.

You probably also have many fears about your parent in jail. You may worry about his or her safety. You may worry about his or her health. There are also many things to fear at home for yourself and the rest of your family. You may be overwhelmed with sadness or anxiety from time to time. But you are not alone.

There are almost a million people in prison in the United States. More than three quarters of the women in prison are parents, and most have more than two children. That means that there are hundreds of thousands of children like you, wondering what will happen to them and to their imprisoned parent.

No matter how difficult things are for you and the rest of your family, remember, *you* did not commit a crime. You should not be punished because your parent did. If people treat you unkindly, as if you are somehow to blame for the actions of your parent, get away from them. Find people to be around who understand what you are going through. Find people who can help you manage this stressful time and make you feel better about yourself.

This book will give you some suggestions about where to turn for help. It will also give you some ideas about how to help yourself. With a strong support system you can learn to deal with whatever happens to you and your family. Don't let the prison your parent is in become a "prison" for you. It will not be easy, but you can survive and get on with the rest of your life.

Chapter 1

Who Goes to Prison?

Jails are usually local facilities run by towns or cities for housing inmates a short time. Prisons are run by states or the federal government. They usually house offenders who are sentenced to terms of more than one year. To simplify things in this book the words "jail" and "prison" are used interchangeably.

There are many slang terms used to describe jails and prisons. You have probably heard words like "stir," "clink," "jug," "can," "pen," "the Big House," or "joint" used in the movies and on television. Often these terms make prison sound like a "hip" place to be. But after you have a closer look at the prison experience and know a little more about the reality of prison, you may find the media portrayal upsetting.

In truth, prison is a frightening place. People in prison lose their most basic freedoms. There is nothing glamorous, fun, or exciting about prison. There are people, however, who manage to live through their experience of prison without giving up on life, who find ways to improve themselves and make the most of a terrible situation.

People from every walk of life, representing every social class—male and female—go to prison. Anyone in our society who commits a crime could end up spending time in jail.

There are more than 800,000 people serving time in prison in the United States. In fact, the United States imprisons a larger part of its population than any other country in the world. And the number of prisoners has been rising steadily in the past 10 years.

Many experts believe this large increase in the number of prisoners is a direct result of a growing drug problem in our society. Illegal drugs bring crime and violence. Also a large share of the prison population is made up of black and Hispanic men and women who are poor and underprivileged.

Consider the following facts:

• In 1989, 29 percent of prisoners in the U.S. were drug offenders. In 1981, only 7.7 percent of prisoners were drug offenders.

• Crime in all major U.S. cities has increased, but between 1981 and 1989, the number of drug-related crimes increased from 11,487 to 87,859.

Some prisons offer inmates educational opportunities. Here, a group of prisoners hold up high-school diplomas after graduation.

- 31.9 percent of U.S. blacks live in poverty.
- 62 percent of black children in the U.S. are born in female-only households.
- 65.3 percent of black single-parent families in the U.S. live in poverty.
- One in three female inmates in the U.S. is in prison for drug-related crime.
- One in four women in prison was convicted of a crime committed to support a drug habit.

Because such a large number of black and Hispanic people in the United States live in poverty, they are at a much higher risk of being involved in a drug-related crime, and being sent to prison because of their involvement. Unfortunately, even today racism can have a strong impact on how crimes are dealt with.

For example, consider the true stories of two different men in the state of New York convicted of the same crime involving possession of drugs with the intent to sell. One man is white. The other is black. In both cases the men were not dealing large quantities of drugs. Their crimes were not considered too serious. In the case of the white man, he was sentenced to two years probation and ordered to enter a drug rehabilitation program. In the case of the black man, he was sent to prison for three years. In fact, in New York State, only 7 percent of drug offenders in prison are white, but white addicts occupy 47 percent of the available spots in state-funded rehab programs.

If he is lucky, the black man may be able to get into a drug rehab program once he is in prison, but there is no guarantee. It is a terrible injustice that one man is offered help and the other is simply shut away based solely on the color of his skin. But discrimination in the system happens over and over again in many different ways.

The combination of crushing poverty, lack of education, and the widespread problem of drug abuse and drug-related crime is part of the reason that such a large proportion of the prison population is made up of minorities.

It is a sad fact that there are many people in prison today who seem better off than they would be if they were out on the street. At least in prison these people have a roof over their heads and food to eat. But no one, no matter how difficult life is on the "outside," enjoys the loss of freedom that comes with imprisonment.

As older prisons become more crowded, other problems arise. There is not enough room to house so many prisoners. In many cases, cafeterias and storage rooms may be turned into dormitories where prisoners sleep. New prisons are badly needed. Taxpayers already spend millions of dollars every year trying to keep up with the growing needs of society. Programs meant to help prisoners, such as drug-treatment programs, halfway houses, and job training, are often cut back for lack of money.

Time Spent in Jail

Every year thousands of people are *incarcerated.* That means they spend some time in prison. Sometimes they are held only a short time; other times it is months or even years.

Usually persons under arrest awaiting trial are allowed to leave jail after paying the *bail* determined by the court. This is money held by the court to assure that the people return to court when it's time for their trial. People who cannot arrange to "put up" bail must stay in prison until their case is tried in court.

After trial, if defendants (persons thought to have committed a crime) are found not guilty of the crime, they are released. If they are found guilty, they are sentenced to prison as punishment. If a person admits to a crime, there is no trial. He or she is sent to jail directly.

In this book you will learn some things about the people who are sent to prison. You will also learn about what can happen to a family when a parent is in prison.

If your parent is in prison for a short time or for many years, you may be feeling afraid about the future for yourself and your family. You may be ashamed that your parent is in prison. Your family will probably go through some very difficult times. Use this book to learn about what is happening to your family. Use this book to understand your situation and to find ways to get help.

Chapter 2

How the System Works

Most people agree that it would be better if there were fewer people in prison. The problem is that there is so much crime. Experts have different opinions about why there is so much crime and what we can do about it. Some people think there should be more programs outside of prisons, like drug-treatment programs, for instance, to help people get their lives in order. Maybe then they would not commit crimes.

Crime

A crime is an unlawful act. Crimes are usually divided into two types, violent crimes (against people) or property crimes. Murder and rape are violent crimes. Shoplifting and vandalism are property crimes. More property crimes are committed each year than violent crimes.

The type of crime a person is accused of committing determines:

- how the crime will be tried in the courts.
- the kind of prison he or she will go to if convicted (minimum or maximum security).
- how long the prison term could be.
- if he or she will be sent to a federal or state prison.

There are more men in prison than women. But the number of women in prison has more than doubled from the early 1980s to the early 1990s. In many cases both men and women ended up in prison because of drugs. They were caught selling, carrying, or using illegal drugs.

Gena's father had deserted the family. Her mother struggled to make ends meet, but times were very hard.

When Gena's mother was fired from her job, things got worse. Gena's mother looked for a new job but couldn't find one. After a while, she stopped looking. One morning she disappeared and didn't come back for days. Gena's mother began using drugs to hide from her problems.

In a short time, Gena's mother became a crack addict. In exchange for drugs and a little extra money, Gena's mother agreed to let some crack pushers deal drugs in her apartment. In her confused state of mind, Gena's mother thought she had found a harmless way to feed her family.

Maximum security prisons have an interior observation center to monitor many cells on several levels.

Gena didn't like having strangers around. It frightened her. Gena was also upset by her mother's strange moods. But at least there was a little money for food. And they still kept their apartment. Gena knew her mother loved her and the other children. "It will be okay," Gena told herself.

That's what Gena thought until the day she came home from school to find the apartment full of police and her mother in handcuffs. A social worker was waiting to take her and her brothers and sisters to foster homes. By that evening, Gena's mother was in jail. It would be a very long time before the family was back together again.

The Arrest

When a person is arrested and taken to jail many things happen. First the person is taken to the police station and "booked" or charged with committing a crime. When a person is arrested he or she loses some rights. But certain rights will remain. These rights are very important. The law says that a person cannot be held in jail unless he or she is accused of a crime. This is why booking takes place as soon as possible.

The person accused of a crime may not be physically hurt or forced to talk. He or she may call a lawyer for advice. The police may have to wait to question the person until the lawyer arrives. Or the person may choose to talk to the police without the lawyer.

The Hearing

The next thing that happens is a hearing. At the hearing a judge is told about the crime. The judge will ask the accused person how he or she pleads, guilty or not guilty. If the person pleads guilty, the judge must then talk with lawyers and decide what the punishment for the crime should be. If the person pleads not guilty, the judge has more to think about.

Sometimes the judge does not think the person has committed a crime or does not think there is enough evidence to prove that a crime has happened. In that case, the judge will dismiss the case and the person is free to go.

At other times, the judge decides that the case should go to trial and schedules a date for the trial. Depending on the type of crime committed, there are different types of trials. (You can find books in your school or public library that explain more about the court system.)

According to the law, the trial must take place as soon as possible. The accused person has a right to know what his or her fate will be. However, the courts are overloaded, and it can take months before a person goes to trial.

Bail

The judge also decides how much bail the person must pay in order to go free until the time of his or her trial. This amount may be very low, only

Some jails are set up more informally than others. Inmates serve shorter sentences for more minor offenses.

a few hundred dollars, or extremely high, as much as a million dollars or more. The amount of bail is usually decided by how serious the crime is and how likely the judge thinks it is that the accused person will try to run away. The more serious the crime and the more evidence against the accused criminal, the higher the bail will be set. Sometimes the judge will not set bail for a particularly dangerous or unpredictable suspect. The person must remain in jail until the trial is over.

Plea Bargaining

After the judge has made a decision, sometimes the accused person, represented by his or her lawyer, will try to bargain with the court to arrange for the person to get out of jail more quickly. This is called plea bargaining. In a plea bargain, the accused person agrees to plead guilty to a less severe crime than the one he or she is accused of committing. In exchange for this plea, the judge decides what the punishment will be and there is no trial.

Since it can take such a long time for a case to go to trial and since a trial can take a long time itself, with no one knowing what the outcome might be, a plea bargain can make things easier on the prisoner. However, not all plea bargains are accepted by the judge.

Sentencing

After the trial, a person may be *acquitted* and set free. This means that the person was found not guilty of committing the crime. In other cases, the person is found guilty, *convicted* of the crime. The next step is called sentencing. During sentencing, the judge decides what the punishment for the crime will be and how long it will last. At this stage a person may be sent to prison, sent to a halfway house, or sent to a treatment program.

A convicted person may also receive a sentence of *probation* for some amount of time. This means that the judge sets certain rules about what the person must do, and not do, in order to stay out of jail. If the person does not live up to the terms of his or her probation, he or she might be sent to prison at a later date.

Parole

During their term in jail, prisoners are watched carefully. Based on the sentence received from the judge, prisoners may be eligible for parole. Parole is an early release from prison. There are usually certain requirements that prisoners must meet to qualify for parole. The prison's parole board decides if a prisoner will be paroled. After release from prison, the prisoner must follow any rules set by the parole board or he or she can be sent back to prison.

Pardon

A pardon is an official early release from prison that happens only under special circumstances. A pardon may be granted, for example, if it is discovered that a person was wrongly imprisoned. It may also be granted if a prisoner becomes extremely ill, or has behaved in an exceptionally honorable way to make up for his or her crime.

Chapter 3

What's It Like in Prison?

There are many different types of prisons. But the one thing they all have in common is that the prisoners are not free to come and go as they please. A *maximum security* prison is for very dangerous criminals who have committed the most serious crimes. These prisoners are kept on a tight schedule. They have a certain amount of time each day to sleep, eat, shower, relax, and exercise. No one goes anywhere without permission.

A *minimum security* prison is structured, but less rigid. Prisoners may have more free time. They may have privileges to go to certain prison areas on their own. They may be able to choose what activities they prefer to participate in.

Most prisons are overcrowded. That means that instead of one person living in a *cell*, there may be two, three, or even four persons sharing a small room. Lounge areas may be converted to sleeping quarters. One of the hardest things prisoners have to deal with is the lack of privacy, no quiet time alone. The more crowded a prison is, the harder it is to have any personal space.

Stresses of Prison Life

Prison is a very stressful place. It is hard for people to get along when they have to live in such cramped quarters. Many people in prison feel lonely and miss their families and friends. They may also be feeling sad, angry, scared, ashamed, or confused. But in prison, it is usually important for prisoners to keep up a brave, tough front. Many inmates do not allow themselves to think about or show their true feelings.

Another cause for stress in prison is the rising epidemic of diseases like AIDS and tuberculosis. As these and other diseases spread among the poorest people in our society, the number of prisoners with serious health problems increases. Although prison officials do their best to keep sick prisoners separated from healthy prisoners, there is no guarantee that the two groups will not have contact with one another. The health risks in prison are frightening to many prisoners.

Anytime people are under a lot of stress they are likely to be short-tempered. It is not surprising that there is a lot of fighting in prison. Sometimes

Outdoor exercise facilities offer prisoners an outlet for stress and a chance to participate in sports.

All meals are eaten at specific times and usually under supervision by prison guards.

tempers flare with angry words, and sometimes there is physical violence. Some prisoners are more troubled than others, while some seem to have control over fellow prisoners. In addition, some inmates have committed more serious crimes than others. And the reasons for the crimes they committed were all different. All things considered, prison can be a very scary place to be.

Help for Prisoners

There are some prisoners for whom jail is a chance at a new life. Time spent in prison may give the person an opportunity to look honestly at his or her past life. It may be a time to make some changes and some hard decisions.

Some prisons have a wide range of programs to help prisoners learn new job skills or learn to be better parents. Literacy programs help prisoners learn to read and write. Substance-abuse programs help prisoners overcome drug or alcohol problems. Counseling can give prisoners a better understanding of what led them to crime in the first place.

There are many kinds of support groups that bring prisoners together. Religious groups and recreational programs—like basketball, baseball, or weight lifting—are also helpful in building up the prisoners' self-esteem. All these programs are intended to provide prisoners with new skills and a new attitude for a happier, more productive life on the outside.

Unfortunately, not all prisons offer good programs. And most prisons do not have enough programs to meet the needs of all the people they must serve. This is because it costs a lot of money to keep these programs running, even though some programs are run by volunteers. It can also be difficult for a prison warden to arrange for the programs to be held in a safe and secure manner that fits in with the prison schedule.

Jesse was excited when he got to the mailbox and saw his father's handwriting on an envelope. It had been several weeks since he'd heard anything about his dad, Patrick. Patrick was in prison. He was serving a 10-year sentence for manslaughter. Patrick had killed someone in a drunk-driving accident. Jesse worried a lot about his dad. His mother didn't want to talk about Patrick anymore. It was like he didn't even exist. But even though Patrick had always had problems because of his drinking, Jesse loved him.

Dear Jesse,

I sure miss you, and your mama. I know she doesn't feel like writing yet, but give her a hug from me. Things here are the same as always. I was hoping to get into the AA program. I've signed up on a list, but there are a lot of names ahead of mine. I know that I'll have a better chance at parole if I can get through the program, but so far I haven't had any luck. It's hard to believe I've been in this place for three years already!

I am taking a class in computers. It's hard, but if I keep at it, maybe by the time I get out of here I'll be able to get a job using what I have learned. There's a rumor going around that they aren't going to continue the computer program after next year. I hope I get down the basics by then.

Take care of yourself and your mama. I love you.

—Dad

Letters from a parent in jail can be reassuring to the rest of the family.

Jesse put down the letter and squeezed his eyes shut. He didn't want to cry—that was for babies. But he missed his dad a lot, and he knew that things must be worse than his dad let on. If Patrick didn't get paroled, Jesse would be 23 years old by the time his dad came home.

Work in Prison

Prisoners may work for pay. The work varies depending on the place. There are jobs that have to do with the operation of the prison itself, like doing prison laundry. There are also other jobs. Some prisons make things, like license plates, or blue jeans that are sold outside of prison. Prisoners are not paid a lot, but they do get an hourly wage. They can use their money to buy things they want (like magazines, cigarettes, or candy), or they may save it, or send it home to their families.

Alternatives to Prison

Halfway houses are a step between prison and home. In a halfway house a prisoner may be allowed to leave for certain periods of time to go to a job or attend school. Sometimes a person may spend several months in a halfway house after being released from prison, before going back to normal life. It can be very hard to get used to living on your own again after prison life. The halfway house can help make the change back a little easier.

A halfway house can also make things easier on a family. A parent who has been away for a long time may be more comfortable seeing his or her children in a halfway house. The halfway house may be close to the prisoner's former home and easy for the family to visit.

Many experts agree that women prisoners, especially those serving time for less serious crimes, ought to be in halfway houses. This way they can see their children regularly and the family is less disrupted. This is not the usual practice, though. It is unfortunate that there are not nearly enough halfway houses available to men or women who would benefit from them.

Another possible alternative to a prison term is house arrest. House arrest means that a person is forced to stay in a particular house or apartment. The prisoner is watched by law-enforcement agents. He or she may have to wear an electronic device that sends a signal that can be followed by a kind of radar or be monitored by computer. This is an unusual situation that occurs only under special circumstances. House-arrest arrangements can be expensive and are usually reserved for those whose sentence is one year or less.

Visits with a parent in jail may have to be conducted by connecting phones while looking through a glass divider.

Chapter 4

Can You See Your Parent?

Maxine was not thrilled to be missing another basketball practice. If she missed one more, the coach had told her she'd be on the bench for the rest of the season. But it had been almost six months since she'd seen her dad. He was 150 miles away.

Maxine's mom had decided that this weekend she would make the long drive to the prison where her husband was serving time. Maxine's father had killed a man in a fight and would be in prison for at least the next seven or eight years. And that was only if he was on good behavior every day and got paroled early.

Maxine was nervous. The drive was boring. She and her mother hardly talked. Maxine tried to get some of her schoolwork done. But she couldn't think about her studies now. She wondered how her dad would look, and what kind of mood he would be in. Finally they reached the prison. They had to stop and sign in at the gate. The guards wore machine guns. Maxine knew that, but it still disturbed her. The whole place was surrounded by high metal fences with barbed wire at the top. The fences had warning signs on them. They were electrified.

When they reached the visitors' parking lot, Maxine's mom said she would wait in the car to give Maxine and her father some time alone. Maxine left her books behind and picked up the small sack of things she had brought along for her dad.

Her stomach was tied in knots. It was worse than the last time she'd visited. Once inside the prison, Maxine had to stop again and wait in line with the other visitors. Everyone had to pass through a metal detector, and the parcels they carried were checked. Maxine always felt like a criminal herself going through all this. When it was her turn, Maxine set her bundle on the table. It went through an x-ray machine like the kind they have at airports, then a guard on the other side of the table looked through it. Maxine walked through a metal detector, too. She was startled as a loud buzzer went off. The guards moved closer and eyed her suspiciously. Maxine stepped back through the detector, held her arms out away from her body and shrugged. She was scared by the staring eyes.

"It's probably your belt buckle," one of the guards said. Maxine quickly pulled it off and set it

This woman is a prisoner at home. A computer monitor and phone are used to check her regularly while she is under house arrest.

on the table. This time the buzzer was silent when she walked through the detector. She breathed a sigh of relief and collected her things.

Maxine followed the other visitors into the lounge where prisoners waited. The lounge was a big room, like a cafeteria. It was painted a dreary color. A few couches lined the walls, but mainly the room was filled with long tables surrounded by chairs. The voices of a dozen prisoners and their visitors filled the room. The fluorescent lighting was very bright.

Maxine's dad waved as soon as she came through the door. She tried hard to smile, but her heart felt as if it would break. Her dad had lost a lot of weight, and more of his hair had turned gray. He had grown a straggly beard that made him look even older. Maxine hurried across the room and gave her dad a big hug. Then she sat down at the table with him and opened up the sack she'd brought. There was a plate of homemade cookies and a photo album. She explained the recent pictures of herself playing basketball and her part in a school play. There were some other shots of Mom around the house. Maxine and her dad looked through the album for a long time, eating cookies and talking. After a while Maxine and her father hugged again and said goodbye. Then Maxine walked back to the car to wait for her mother. She managed to keep a straight face until the car door slammed and she was alone. Then she cried.

A Long Way from Home

One of the greatest hardships for families and prisoners is the fact that the two are usually separated by a long distance. Most prisons are built in isolated areas. This is for the security of the prison and the safety of others. Being set apart from the community makes it more difficult for prisoners to escape. It is also true that most people do not want a prison in their neighborhood. This distance may make the separation even more painful for the families of prisoners.

A Space for Family Life

In some prison compounds there are special arrangements made to house families during visits. Some areas have organizations that help families to get to see an imprisoned mother or father. The organization may arrange bus rides and special activities like barbecues, picnics, and parties for the families.

In California, and some other states, there are several prisons that have actually set up special camp areas with small trailer homes for families. Families can live together in the trailer homes, as a regular family, for up to two weeks. Of course, this service is an option only for prisoners who are considered to be minimum security risks with minimum sentences. There are still restrictions, and the family must abide by prison regulations while living in the camp.

Many women's prisons have nursery facilities so a new mother can bond with her child immediately after birth.

However, it is a healthy and positive opportunity for families to be together in a more "normal" setting. The camp gives the family a chance to talk, have meals together, and just hang out.

Some prisons have children's centers where mothers and children can spend the day together. The centers give the family time and space to enjoy one another and a way to try to cope with the difficulty of living apart.

At the Bedford Hills Correctional Facility for Women in New York, there is a very special children's center where mothers and their children can play games, read stories, eat, have fun together, and even take naps. The prison also allows women inmates to keep their newborn babies with them and offers classes to teach prison mothers how to be better parents. Many of the women find the programs a great help and feel they are able to improve their relationships with their children as a result of the classes.

Remember, every prison is different. You need to find out whether or not special services are available for families of prisoners at the prison where your parent is serving time. Local organizations to help prisoners' families can also give you information about this. (Check the Where to Get Help section at the end of this book.) Some prisons even have family counseling sessions where all members of the family are able to talk about how they feel.

Some prisons have workshop programs to help interested inmates learn new skills.

A Hard Time for Families

All prisons have regular visiting times, but not all prisons have strong support systems or outside help. In many cases, the family must pay their own way to get to the prison. Since so many of the families with an imprisoned parent are poor, this kind of expense is very hard on the family. In fact, it may be impossible for the family to go for a visit at all. Many families cannot afford to rent a car, buy bus or train tickets, and pay for food and a hotel.

Seeing your parent will depend on many things besides your family's ability to pay for the necessary arrangements. It will depend on the nature of the crime your parent committed, the type of prison he or she is in, and your age. When you

39

visit a parent, you need to find out what the rules and regulations are about visiting and what, if any, programs are available to help.

You can call the prison *warden* to get help. He or she is the person responsible for running the prison. Or you might try contacting the prison *chaplain* (priest or minister), who often arranges for support groups and other programs to help prisoners. There may also be a special department in the prison that handles visits from the outside for families who have special needs. You may feel more comfortable asking someone to help you contact the prison where your parent is. That is also a good way to find out what resources are available.

Phone Calls

Visits are not the only thing that can be difficult and expensive for families of prisoners. Prison phone systems are not set up like your phone at home. It may cost the inmates of the prison a lot to call out, and time spent on the phone is limited. Many prisons allow phone calls only if they are charged to the person receiving the call. That usually makes the call more expensive. There are newer phone systems available today that aren't so expensive, but only very few prisons have actually installed them.

Chapter 5

Changes in the Family

Your family may be affected in many different ways when a parent goes to jail. These changes may last only a short while. Or things may never be the same for your family. In either case, you and your family may need help in finding ways to cope with new problems.

Money Troubles

One of the most immediate effects that a parent's going to jail will have on your family is a shortage of money. If the parent who goes to jail is the main wage earner in your family, that income is lost. It is possible that your family will get money from the government for rent and food stamps but that may not be the case in all situations.

Lawyers and court costs are expensive, too. Sometimes a person who commits a crime not only goes to jail, but is also sued for some reason. If the crime your parent committed hurt someone or damaged property, the person who was injured or whose property was damaged might file a lawsuit and ask the court for compensation (payment) for the injury or loss suffered.

Carey was tired of packing alone. Her sister had gone out to the porch to be with her boyfriend.

Carey's dad was in prison. He had been caught making fake sales of expensive houses, antiques, and paintings to people in town. The kids at school joked about Carey's "con artist dad." The recent newspaper stories about the father's crimes and his trial had embarrassed the whole family. To make matters worse, the people her father had tricked were now suing him. Everything the family owned had been taken away. Their cars had been sold; their house and even their furniture was gone.

Carey, her sister, and her mother were packing up their few belongings and moving to California to live with Carey's grandmother. Carey was scared, sad, and angry. She hated her father for doing this to all of them. At the same time, she missed him. She worried about him, too. When they moved, she wouldn't be able to see him at all. It would be at least two years before he could be released from prison. By then, Carey wondered if she'd even care.

With one parent in jail, families may have to move to less expensive housing or move in with a relative.

New Ways to Live

When a family's financial situation changes and suddenly they have much less money, other things change, too. It may be necessary to move to a smaller place or to move in with relatives. Or it may be necessary for the family to split up while the free parent searches for work or a better place to live. If you are the child of a single parent who is sent to jail, you may end up living with relatives or living with a foster family. Sometimes brothers and sisters are are allowed to stay together with the same foster family, but that is not always possible.

Blame and Guilt

Money problems are not the only reasons that children may have to live in foster homes. In some cases, the parent who was sent to jail may have been abusive and harmed his or her spouse. In a case like this, the court may remove the children from the home if it is not sure that the remaining parent is capable of caring for the children.

It is painful and frightening to be taken away from one's parents. You may feel homesick and lonely. Or you may feel guilty. Even though what happens is not your fault, many children think that they are to blame somehow for the bad things that happen in their family. *Your parent alone is responsible for his or her own actions.* Your parent's bad choices have nothing to do with you. It is very important to remember this.

Stress

It may be that when one of your parents is sent to prison, the rest of the family will be able to stay together. You may even be able to stay in the same house. Life may seem pretty much the same as it was before. But the stress of knowing that your parent is a criminal may still cause you a lot of emotional pain. You may feel depressed, confused, or angry. The other members of your family will probably have similar feelings, but they may try to hide their feelings. Each family member will cope in his or her own way. All of you will need time to adjust. And some of you may also need professional counseling.

Dealing with Shame

Lizzie didn't want to go to school, but her foster mother insisted. She had reminded Lizzie that it wouldn't get any easier to show her face at school if she waited a few more days or even weeks. Lizzie would only be more behind in her school work. No matter what, when she went back to school, the kids were going to make it hard for her.

Two days before, Lizzie's mother and father had been arrested after they had a terrible fight. Everyone in the neighborhood had heard the yelling and swearing and had seen them both being dragged from the house by the police. Lizzie called her grandmother, but she had had enough of Lizzie's parents and of Lizzie, too. Lizzie was living with Mrs. Stokes

Embarrassment and shame may cause feelings of isolation.

until the judge decided whether or not to dismiss the charges against one of her parents. Her mother had filed charges against Lizzie's father. He had filed charges against his wife. The truth was, and Lizzie knew because she'd seen the whole thing, they had both been beating up on each other.

So now, as Lizzie was walking to school, she felt sick to her stomach and her head was aching. She had promised Mrs. Stokes that she would face the kids in class despite her shame, but at the last minute she lost her nerve. Instead she spent the day wandering around the mall until it was time to go home. Maybe tomorrow she'd be able to walk back into her high school.

Shame is an uncomfortable feeling. No one likes to experience it. Shame is a feeling that makes you want to hide from other people. It can make you feel worthless and bad. When a person does something seriously wrong, we often think that he or she should feel ashamed. We want the person to be reminded that his or her behavior was not acceptable.

Most people feel ashamed at one time or another. Have you ever done something that you wish you hadn't done? Cheated on a test? Taken money from your mom's purse? Lied to your folks about where you were? Feeling ashamed in these situations is probably a good thing. It reminds you that you made a mistake and need to correct your behavior. But sometimes people like Lizzie feel ashamed of things that they have no control over. You can tell yourself over and over that you did nothing wrong, but having a parent in jail can still make you feel ashamed. You may need help to understand why you are being so hard on yourself.

A Hard View

Society as a whole reacts badly to people who are accused of crimes and worse to people who are actually convicted of crimes. It is very hard, for example, for people who have been imprisoned to get work. Even if their crimes were not serious, often society feels it cannot trust former convicts again. This attitude may seem unfair because many people pay their debt to society and continue to live a crime-free life.

Your community may try to make *you* feel bad if your parent's crime was widely reported. If the crime your parent committed was violent, people may actually behave as if they are afraid of you! Remember, their behavior is wrong. You are not the guilty party. You did not commit a crime. You do not in any way deserve their cruel behavior. But it is important to know that they may treat you unkindly. Try to prepare yourself. It may happen often or only once. But when it does happen, it will hurt. If you plan in advance how you will respond, you may be better able to handle the pain.

Chapter 6

Finding Support

Y ou will have a lot of confusing feelings about your parent in jail. You will probably feel angry sometimes, wondering why your parent committed a crime and left you. You will feel sad at all the strange things happening in your life. It will be embarrassing sometimes to face other people when they know that your parent is in jail. You may also feel lonely and miss your parent a lot. All of these feelings are normal. You will sometimes feel many different things all at once.

You may also feel guilty. There may be other things in your life to feel guilty about, but you should not feel guilty about your parent's punishment. It is very important to remind yourself of this. That is especially difficult if something you did helped to send your parent away. But even if you were the one to call the police when your father was beating your mother, or if your parent committed a crime against you and you pressed charges, it is still not your fault that your parent is in jail. THE REASON YOUR PARENT IS IN JAIL IS BECAUSE HE OR SHE COMMITTED A CRIME.

You are not responsible in any way. You did not commit a crime. You did what you *had* to do to protect yourself or your family. It will be hard enough to get on with your life just dealing with the outside world. Don't let unnecessary guilt make it worse. If you feel guilty or responsible in any way for what your parent is going through, STOP! Find someone who can help you to see things more clearly.

There are many places where you can find help getting through this very stressful time. Look through the Where to Get Help section at the end of this book. If you cannot find the name of a group that might meet your exact needs, call some of them anyway. Many of these organizations are run by people who have direct experience with what you are going through. Some of them may have been prisoners themselves. They will understand your fears and concerns. If they cannot help you themselves, they may be able to tell you about another group that can.

Friends may offer support and give advice for helping to cope with difficult situations.

The Personal Touch

You should also try to talk with someone you
can really trust, a friend, teacher, another family
member, or a social worker. You need someone
who will take the time to listen. You need to be
able to express all of your feelings safely. You may
need to be reassured by those who know you and
care about you.

If your family is religious, try talking with someone in your church or temple. Remember that
there are people around who will open their arms
and help you. Try to surround yourself with
people who believe in you and your ability to deal
with your problems.

What to Do about Your Parent in Jail

How do you feel about your parent in jail? What
has he or she done to you and your family? Can you
forgive your convicted parent? Do you want him or
her back in your life? It is important to think about
these questions, but not to be controlled by them.
You need to understand your feelings so you can be
free to make your own choices.

In addition to counseling, keeping a journal may
be helpful, too. You can write down your most
private feelings concerning your parent and how
his or her going to jail has changed your life. You
will not be judged or feel any pressure. You may
want to write letters to your parent that you don't
send. This freedom to express your feelings may

help you to "let go" of your scared and angry feelings. It may be a necessary step for you before you have any direct contact with your parent in jail.

Keeping in Touch

If you have a good relationship with your parent and you want to keep in touch, there are several things you can do. Write letters. Make video or audio tapes to give your parent an idea of how the family is doing. Visit if you can. Get involved in any family programs the prison may offer. Keep a family journal or scrapbook to record important events that occur while your parent is away. All these ways may help you to keep the relationship between your parent and yourself alive.

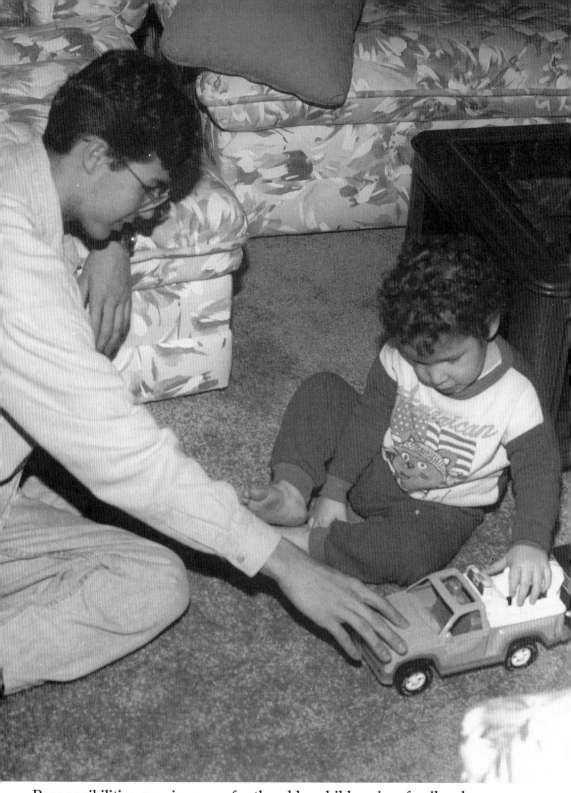

Responsibilities may increase for the older children in a family when one parent is in jail.

Chapter 7

Looking Ahead

It is hard to be the child of a parent in jail. On top of everything else, it may have caused you to take on many extra responsibilities. You may have younger brothers and sisters who look to you for comfort. And your parent at home also may turn to you for help. You may feel unable or unwilling to handle all that is expected of you.

Home Again

Depending on the type of crime your parent was imprisoned for, he or she will be returning home in a matter of months or years. Some parents may want to pretend that once they are home everything will be the same as it was before. But that is not realistic. Things will be different. Even if you and your parent have kept in touch, you both will need time to get reacquainted. Your life has been affected in many ways by your parent's time in jail.

You may have learned new things about yourself. You may feel proud that you were able to help your family when they needed you. Or, you may be resentful that your life had to change because of your parent's absence. It may take a while before your parent truly understands all that you have experienced.

If you did not have a good relationship with your parent before, or if his or her crime was directed at you or your family, you may have serious fears about dealing with your parent when he or she is released from prison. You may not want him or her to return, and you may be angry at your other parent for taking the imprisoned parent back. These are more issues to be discussed in family counseling sessions.

Your parent also may have a lot of confusing feelings. He or she may feel unwelcome at home and in the community. He or she may not know what to do to make things better. It is important for both of you to talk honestly and openly about your feelings. You and your family need to find healthy ways to deal with the past and to move ahead with your lives.

Being at Risk

Through all this adjustment, it is very important to remember that YOU did not do anything wrong. YOU are not responsible for the crime your parent committed or was accused of committing. And,

A warm welcome for the returning parent can be a new beginning for a reunited family.

most important, the fact that your parent committed a crime and ended up in jail does *not* mean that you will, too.

It is a sad fact that many of the children of parents who are prisoners will someday be in jail themselves. In fact, children of prisoners are five times more likely to be imprisoned themselves than children of parents who never went to prison. But this has a lot to do with the problems faced by children who are left without parents, without enough money, and without any guidance.

If you are worried about the possibility that you too might commit a crime someday and end up in jail, take steps *now* in your life to avoid making bad choices. You can take advantage of the many programs that exist to help young people. Talk to counselors about your fears. Learn to work through your anger and develop better self-esteem. Set goals for yourself like learning new job skills or advancing your education.

The problems and mistakes of your parent have had an effect on your life. And even if you have been hurt by those mistakes, you can try to learn from them. You can try to remain positive about your own life. There is no need to be afraid to ask for help. You owe it to yourself to make your own choices and be happy.

Glossary—*Explaining New Words*

acquittal Court decision that says a person is not legally responsible for a crime he or she was accused of committing.

AIDS (acquired immunodeficiency syndrome) Viral disease that damages the immune system so that the body is open to many infections. It is transmitted by sexual activity and by sharing of unclean hypodermic needles in drug use.

bail Money paid so that an accused person may be released from jail until the court has decided the case.

cell Living quarters of a prisoner; a small room.

convicted (of a crime) Found guilty of committing a crime.

court Place where legal matters are decided.

halfway house Place for helping people adjust to society after being imprisoned or hospitalized.

incarcerate Put in prison.

judge Person who decides legal matters in court.

jury Group of people who hear facts about a crime and with the help of the judge determine if the accused person is guilty or not guilty of the crime.

parole Early release from prison based on certain conditions that the prisoner must follow.

plea Accused person's answer to being charged with a crime, for example, guilty or not guilty.

plea bargain Agreement between an accused person and the court that the person will plead guilty to a less serious crime in order to receive a lighter punishment.

probation Alternative to prison; a person guilty of a crime must be supervised and agree to certain conditions (for example, entering a drug treatment program) in order to remain free.

sentencing Pronouncing the judge's decision about how a convicted person will be punished.

trial Examination of facts to determine whether a person is guilty or not guilty of a crime.

tuberculosis Disease of the lungs transmitted especially between people living in close quarters.

under arrest Held in legal custody.

Where to Get Help

In addition to the organizations listed, check your local Yellow Pages or call your State or County Social Services Department for help in your area.

Bureau of Prisons
320 First Street, NW
Washington, D.C. 20534
(202) 307-3198

The Fortune Society
39 West 19th Street
New York, NY 10011
(212) 206-7070

**Prison Families
  Anonymous**
c/o The Fortune Society

**The Children's Center
  (Bedford Hills
  Correcional Facility)**
247 Harris Road
Bedford Hills, NY 10507
(914) 241-3100

The Women's Jail Project
P.O. Box 1592
Madison, WI 53701-1592

Horizon House
1869 North 25th Street
Milwaukee, WI 53205

**Catholic Community
  Services, L.I.F.T.
  Program**
P.O. Box 70
Alderson, WV 24910
(304) 445-2617

**The Program for Female
  Offenders**
1520 Penn Avenue
Pittsburgh, PA 15222
(412) 281-7380

JusticeWorks Community
1012 8th Avenue
Brooklyn, NY 11215
(718) 499-6704

Institute of Women Today
73115 S. Yale
Chicago, IL 60621
(312) 651-8372

**Chicago Legal Aid to
  Incarcerated Mothers
  (CLAIM)**
205 Randolph Street
Chicago, IL 60606
(312) 332-5537

For Further Reading

Budal, Charlotte. "Behind No Bars." *Children Today*, May 1990, pages 30–33.

Church, George. "The View from Behind Bars." *Time*, Fall 1990, pages 20–22.

Creighton, Linda. "Nursery Rhymes and Hard Times." *U.S. News and World Report*, August 8, 1988, pages 33–34.

Hjelmeland, Andy. "Is a Rap Sheet a Legacy?" *Newsweek*, May 15, 1989, page 10.

Huje, Virginia. "Mom's in Prison: Where Are the Kids?" *Progressive*, April 1992, pages 22–23.

Lerner, Stephen. "Women Behind Bars." *Cosmopolitan*, June, 1989, pages 214–217.

Check your library for books and other magazine articles about families coping with a parent in prison. Ask your librarian about a magazine called *Corrections Today.* It deals with many prison issues that will help you to learn more about the prison system and the changing programs within it.

Index

About the Author

Stephanie St. Pierre is the author of more than thirty books for children, including *Jim Henson, Creator of the Muppets*, *The Story of the Star-Spangled Banner*, and *Everything You Need to Know When a Parent Is Out of Work*. She has also written fiction for children of all ages. Ms. St. Pierre lives with her husband and two children in New York. She is the editorial director of a children's book publisher, and an artist in her spare time.

Acknowledgments and Photo Credits

Cover photo: Dick Smolinski.
Photos on pages 2, 11, 37, 39: AP/Wide World Photos; pages 20, 25, 26, 32, 35: Gamma-Liaison; page 17: © Pierre Perrin/Gamma Liaison; pages 29, 43, 51, 54, 57: Stuart Rabinowitz.

Design/Production: Blackbirch Graphics, Inc.